MW01075436

Letter
Birds

Illustrated by
Pam Spremulli

PublishingWorks, Inc.
2009

PublishingWorks, Inc.,
151 Epping Road
Exeter, NH 03833
603-778-9883

For Sales and Orders:

1-800-738-6603 or 603-772-7200
LCCN: 2009937685
ISBN-13: 978-1-935557-56-2

Printed in the United States.
Second Printing, October 2010.

www.pamspremulli.com

For Ella and Mai
My inspired little birds

Aa
Akepa

Bb
Bluebird

Cc

Cardinal

Dd
Duck

Ee
Egret

Ff

Flamingo

Gg

Goldfinch

Hh
Hummingbird

Ii

Ibis

Jj

Jackdaw

Kk
Kingfisher

Ll

Lapwing

Mm
Magpie

Nn
Nuthatch

Oo

Owl

Pp
Pheasant

Qq

Quail

Rr
Robin

Ss
Sparrow

Tt
Towhee

Uu
Umbrella Bird

Vv
Vireo

Ww

Woodpecker

Xx
Xenops

Yy

Yellowthroat

Zz

Zenaida Dove

The
End

The only thing more cheerfully optimistic than Pam Spremulli is her art. Most well known for her unique interpretations of architectural landmarks from New England to New Orleans, Pam takes familiar images and manipulates color in a way that's eye catching and engaging. In "Letter Birds", she proves that her skills are lent equally as well to the world of nature.

Born and raised in the Chautauqua Lake Region of Western, NY, Pam finds herself very much at home with this subject and instinctively draws the viewers eye to key points of a species that might go unnoticed with more traditional forms of art.

Pam is a graduate of Niagara University and is a graphic designer, accredited by the School of the Museum of Fine Arts, Boston, MA.

She resides in Chagrin Falls, Ohio with her husband David, daughters Ella and Maizie, and her many bird friends.